To My
Country

Author's Note

About mid-December 2019 it became clear to me that Australia was in an unprecedented bushfire crisis. I was preparing to spend another Christmas away from home, which wasn't entirely unusual. I'd lived away from Australia for twelve years but had tried to come back for Christmas when I could. I've never really enjoyed a Christmas spent away from my family, but Christmas 2019 was particularly difficult. I felt, as many Aussie expats all over the world felt, like I should be there in our country's time of dire need. To do what, I'm not entirely sure.

By New Years Eve the situation in Australia was worldwide news and all I could think about. I woke up on the morning of January 1st 2020 feeling none of the usual hope or promise that a new year brings. I felt despair. And anger. At some point in the first week of January I sat down to try to wrest some of this onto paper. I recorded myself reading my poem in the kitchen of my Vancouver apartment and uploaded it to social media.

The response was immediate and overwhelming. And it confirmed what I already knew in my heart: the bond we as Australians have to our country is more powerful than any disaster we face. We will overcome. In a world consumed with the making of money, I think and hope we are finally realising that the earth is all we really have.

—Ben Lawson, 2020

All royalties earned by the purchase of this book
are generously donated by the author to

The Koala Hospital

which since 1973 has been rescuing, treating,
rehabilitating, releasing and educating the world about
one of Australia's most iconic and most vulnerable species.

To My Country

Ben Lawson

with illustrations by Bruce Whatley

ALLEN&UNWIN

SYDNEY · MELBOURNE · AUCKLAND · LONDON

This book is dedicated to all the firefighters
who fought and continue to fight to protect our land
and every living thing that inhabits it

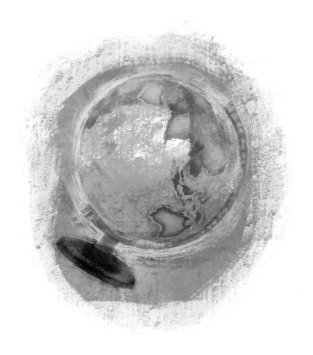

The place I'm from is far away;
she's wide and flat and brown.
When looking at a globe she's
the one just under and down.

She raised me up and taught me almost
everything I know.
Like how to live and how to love;
she's how I learned to grow.

And though I had no say in where
my folks chose to reside,
I always sort of had a sense
of patriotic pride.

I'd always felt connected from
a space somewhere within.
See that's the thing about this place:
she gets under your skin.

So when the time had come after
two decades and a half
to go and see the world, she didn't
scoff, she didn't laugh.

She understood I had so much
I needed to explore.
And that I would return, for she
had seen my kind before.

And so I ventured out and joined
an inauspicious posse
of dreamers living far from home:
expatriated Aussies.

The streets of Brooklyn, London's Eye,
an Indonesian Sizzler.
Cafes in Paris, tratts in Rome,
or every shop in Whistler.

You hear our voices everywhere
like members of a club.
Fanning out across the world,
quite often in a pub.

We smile when people mimic us,
quote Crocodile Dundee.
To them we sound absurd; I guess
we do to a degree.

They talk about the snakes and sharks
as if it's some big fuss.
'I couldn't live down there!' they say.
We say, 'That's fine by us.'

Somehow the months turn into several
trips around the sun.
Yet that tie to the motherland's
as strong as on day one.

Regardless though, how far away
I happen to have wandered,
I need to check to see who won
the Hottest of the Hundred.

I'll always find a pub to watch
the Granny on the telly.
And four days before Christmas I
will always play Paul Kelly.

It really doesn't matter just
how far or wide I roam.
The Boy from Oz was right I guess:
it's never not your home.

And when I cross another Aussie
travelling awhile,
we'll nod and say g'day and then
we'll share a knowing smile.

You see, we know it matters really
not that much at all
if England takes The Ashes home
or World Cup hopes are small.

Perhaps we won't win quite as many
medals as the Yanks.
At Wimbledon we might not have
a top ten in the ranks.

'Cause we've still got the greatest gift,
a wonder all its own —
a paradise of sand and sun
we get to call our home.

I think about her often, and
that feeling comes along:
that warm familiar pride that tells
me she's where I belong ...

and Crowded House comes on in some
strange far-flung foreign bar.
My eyes sting for a moment. Man,
sometimes I feel so far.

The purpose of these verses though
is not to hear me muse.
But rather what I saw that day
when opening the news.

Austral on fire

- Helicopters and naval vessels deplo...
- Military called in to help emergency
- New South Wales fire Commissi...

My heart stopped for a second and
my throat became too tight.
Her name was in the headlines and
she didn't look alright.

I had to sit, I couldn't quite
believe my own two eyes.
She looked unrecognisable;
I'd never seen those skies.

Not in the place where I grew up,
that's not what I remember.
Bushfires never started up so
early as September.

It's much too much to fathom that
your homeland could succumb
to such a horror. And they said,
the worst was yet to come.

I watched as towns evacuated,
stared as children choked.
New Zealand looked on helplessly
through black and acrid smoke.

A single fire, big as Belgium,
turned the skies vermilion,
and helpless wildlife vanished 'til
we'd lost more than a billion.

'Don't be afraid,' they tell us, 'of
a little Aussie coal.
This stuff is worth a fortune, it's
like carbonised black gold!'

'So what if it's not great in an environmental sense.
Just think of the economy!
Don't focus on science.'

'Now's not the time to talk about
our planet getting hotter,
or fire seasons lengthening
or folks who don't have water.'

'It's sad we lost some good people,
a firey or three.
At least they died knowing we've got
a healthy GDP.'

I mustered that old Aussie pride,
but to my disbelief
discovered only anger there
and overwhelming grief.

We say we love our country, but
that leaves a bitter taste.
Our apathy to climate change
should make us feel disgraced.

We're so concerned with digging up that black stuff from the ground. Myself, I'd rather have those billion animals around.

But then I saw the photos of
dark figures in the fray.
Those tiny silhouettes fighting
to keep the flames at bay.

I read about the volunteers
who never got a Chrissy.
Just threw themselves into the blaze
from Adelaide to Brissy.

I read in awe about our fearless
firefighting crews,
who could've thrown the towel in any
time, but they refused.

Our men and women out there in
the midst of devastation,
upon their yellow jackets pinned
the soft prayers of a nation.

I watched as ordinary Aussies
rose to the occasion.
Feeding precious animals half-
dead from dehydration.

They sent in cash and clothes and food
to those who'd lost it all.
And kids were even chipping in
with cupcakes at a stall.

And suddenly I got the pang
from somewhere deep inside.
The one that starts down in my gut
and rises like a tide.

The same one that runs through me,
putting fire in my veins.
It now glowed deep within and so
much brighter than those flames.

And though I found myself so far
away when she was ailing,
I know I've never been so proud
to call myself Australian.

Thank you

One of the people who reached out to me after seeing this poem online was a lady by the name of Kelly Fagan. She said she worked for a publishing company in Sydney and thought it would make a beautiful illustrated book; due solely to her determination, you now hold that book in your hands. Thank you, Kelly, this is a big deal for me. Thank you to Bruce Whatley, whose timeless illustrations elevated this book beyond anyone's expectations. He was my first and only choice, and I still can't believe he agreed to do it. Thank you to Kirby Armstrong, who is responsible for the overall design of this book, including the stunning cover. My sincere and eternal gratitude to Dolly, Tim, Stephen, Julia and Barry for your gracious words. And to Courtney Lick, who expertly pulled all these elements together at the eleventh hour. Thanks to my agent, Trish McAskill, who worked with me throughout the publishing process: a new one for both of us! And finally to my mum, Dianne, who has been there for every high and so many lows, whose faith in me is irrepressible and who I know will proudly show off this book to all her friends, especially now that I've put her in the acknowledgements.

About the Author

Ben Lawson grew up in Brisbane, one of five boys. He studied acting at NIDA and worked in theatre throughout Sydney and Melbourne.

He has been based in Los Angeles since 2008 where he has acted extensively in television shows, such as *Firefly Lane*, *Modern Family*, *The Good Place*, *Billions*, *Thirteen Reasons Why* and *Designated Survivor*, and films, including *Bombshell* and *No Strings Attached*.

Ben misses being in the ocean at Noosa, eating chicken burgers in North Bondi and watching live music on balmy St Kilda nights, as well as a million other things he used to take for granted.

To My Country is his first book.

About the Illustrator

Bruce Whatley took the plunge into picture books in 1992. Over 90 books later, he is a much-loved and much-awarded illustrator with beloved characters such as Wombat, a Very Ugly Dog and the Little Refugee seen on bookshelves across the world.

In 2008, he completed his PhD thesis *Left Hand Right Hand: Implications of ambidextrous image making* and has since illustrated four books with his non-dominant left hand.

Bruce constantly innovates unique ways to tell a story and to entertain and surprise the reader. For this book, he developed a new style to meet a very tight schedule and to reflect the sentiment of Ben's emotional text. The illustrations were produced in Procreate on an iPad using multiple layered textures and drawing with the eraser tool to remove the spaces between the objects and characters.

Bruce lives on the South Coast of NSW.

First published in 2020

Copyright © Ben Lawson 2020

Illustration copyright © Bruce Whatley 2020

Allen & Unwin
83 Alexander Street
Crows Nest NSW 2065
Australia
Phone: (61 2) 8425 0100
Email: info@allenandunwin.com
Web: www.allenandunwin.com

 A catalogue record for this
book is available from the
National Library of Australia

ISBN 978 1 76087 871 9

Cover and internal design by Kirby Armstrong
Set in 29/35 pt Tooth & Nail
Printed by C & C Offset Printing Co., Ltd, China

10 9 8 7 6 5 4 3 2 1